PAINTED BLUE
WITH SALTWATER

Also by Logan February

How to Cook a Ghost (Glass Poetry Press)

PAINTED BLUE WITH SALTWATER

LOGAN FEBRUARY

© 2018 Logan February

Cover photographs: Lisa Gilman
cover design: adam b. bohannon
Book design: Nieves Guerra
Book editor: Samantha Pious

Published by Indolent Books,
an imprint of Indolent Art Foundation, Inc.

www.indolentbooks.com
Brooklyn, New York
ISBN: 978-1-945023-08-8

This book is dedicated to the memory of my father,
and to the water, because sometimes blood is not enough.

CONTENTS

On Fridays, I Let Myself Hope 11

We Are Your Children 12

Self-Portrait as a Child Who Isn't Yours 13

Feeble Attempts at Thaumaturgy 15

A Night of No New Things 16

Are You Fucking the One You Love 17

Self-Portrait With Foreign Tongue 18

In the Light of the Prayer Room 19

Crying as a Sacred Ritual 20

Self-Portrait as Rainbow Boy 21

To Worship Pollution 22

Picaresque 23

Self-Portrait as a Study in Asphyxia 24

The Ghost of Valentino 25

Tea With My Grandmother 26

On Fathers & Boiling Water 29

Self-Portrait as Victim of Bug Spray 30

Self-Portrait as Pussyboy 31

Kuebiko 32

Ixora 33

Fleas 34

Hope is a Box of Bees 35

Black Hoodie, Wolfboy, Heartache 36

Lonesome Bodies 37

Learning to Float 38

Even the Birds 39

TFW You Are Just A Roadmap 40

Stillbirth, Yemoja 41

The Bodies of Dead Boys 42

Self-Portrait as a Safe House by the Sea 43

Acknowledgments 45

About the Author 47

About Indolent Books 47

> Between what I want
> and what I want to be, I get a little lost.
> —Sonya Vatomsky

> most days i feel i am walking through water
> most days i forget the sound of my voice
> —Safia Elhillo

On Fridays, I Let Myself Hope

Dragon eyes are watching me
& my home is no sanctuary.

I've built myself boxes out of
bird bones & rosary beads.

My mother complains about
the secrets that I keep in them.

I was born with my skin tattooed
in a dead language, infernal to translate.

The child in the crib
with bats hanging off the frame

is calling his diseased mind
the devil himself.

How open my mouth must be,
to name things I have never seen.

The underside of my tongue is rancid
with rot and words;

my mother complains about being in the dark—
I complain of being born with it.

On Fridays, I grow leathery wings,
& when the devil takes me dancing,

I pretend he is all the boys I have ever loved.

We Are Your Children

This is his bedroom, where his body
houses a dead version of itself.

At night, in the dark,
he will take a screwdriver to his ribs

to scratch someone else's name
into them, one by one,

until they believe him
& then he believes himself.

All the scales are on the floor.
The skin is shed too early

& still he does not look
like his brothers.

The family photograph reveals all of
the undressed bodies beneath the floors.

A house is a box of doors,
of openings, of wounds.

Self-Portrait as a Child Who Isn't Yours

In a dream I am eight days old and
my mother has not tasted salt since I was born.
There is a custom of looking at the house
before giving a name to the child.

My father is a rooted man, my mother
made of water; my siblings little mud huts,
looking at a baby they do not yet know
is an outsider. They pin a word to my body
that translates into

this is what God wanted to happen

and they are wrong in a way that is tragic.
I am the brother who is made of air—
they are cradling a homeless child.

I wake to a clenched fist asking
if my hand is a remedy
or a wither waiting to cascade

does my name translate to
{grief}   or   {abomination}

am I an antonym for what God wanted
to happen   am I the opposite of what

my family named me   & am I the one
to blame   for their unknowing

When I say I am not
a citizen of dreams,
what I mean is:

the only other dream I have is the one
in which my mother now calls me
that dreadful boy.

Feeble Attempts at Thaumaturgy

I am not a miracle-worker, cannot stop
a sunset from bleeding to night.

Darkness only ever collapses inward.
The owls in my room have ceased speaking.

I'm curling myself into the tree branches.
I want to be attached to something

that is also attached to something. Apathy
cradles me, a mother I did not ask for.

I've worn thin all of the skin on my face,
tearing temples to the ground

& still remaining the unsacred
exception to all of the rules.

Bitterness is the myth I left in my mouth &
did not remember to swallow.

Fairy boy is lonely boy every weekend.
The night opens itself, a crocus.

A Night of No New Things

Dissolve two fallen stars in a cup of chamomile
and it tastes a lot like sweet deception.

Tell me, how does it hurt
to never catch your breath even after
you spend the whole night running?

I have gone swimming with sea monsters,
I have gone swimming in sand buckets,
teaching myself to breathe Neptune air
with Nigerian lungs—
I will tell you how the resignation
rolls off my solar-panel skin
as I play Rochambeau with my shadow
paper, scissors, look at my pieces.

Morning light brought the birdsong,
and they came here to find me.

I've left my body
to go haunting sandcastles.

Tell me, how does it hurt
to never really reach yourself?

Are You Fucking the One You Love

There is an old song about hurting
& it plays in your head when he walks by you.

New-month melancholia
about emptiness that

stings & rings
& resonates.

All you know about him is
his name is Marcus & his hands are soft.

You leave your fingerprints in the wrong places
when you have to fold your wings under a shirt.

Heart palpitations come in time
with the ticking of the grandfather clock.

The nymph has dark-blue skin
& eyes for you.

She is the mask that gnaws on your face,
makes you pendulum-swing,

this way & that. This way
you stay undiscovered & that is that.

Your ankles are hard to manage
in these moments,

but at least your bed is warm at night,
and you are fucking somebody.

Self-Portrait With Foreign Tongue

We speak only in echoes &
echoes are not a language of youth.

I am unlearning this
dead dialect, this art of

lifting head & lifting hands
with nothing to lift the spirit,

of opening myself like a door
that leads nowhere in particular.

I sit & watch my skin fall off.
Some hymns are sung for far too long.

In the Light of the Prayer Room

There are questions like
where does the sun go at night
and then there are questions like
how do you define a room full of emptiness,

the answers of which can only be tasted
in a bite of nectarine, or in the kiss
of a fairy you are in love with.

I could say the sun goes with him,
Marcus, the marijuana boy.
He talks about flying and walks
like he floats.
He is left-handed so he must be
out of this world.

Every night, he leaves, and the light
morphs into batwing—
the sky being too vast
for the stars to leave footprints in.

As for rooms,
they are best left with the windows
open & the curtains drawn. The empty is
just another feature, like lintels.

Where I pray
is the kind of room
whose walls should be painted blue
with saltwater.

Crying as a Sacred Ritual

to be filled with the spirit
is to slant yourself   like sunlight
on yellowing leaves
hold your wrists so they look
like an afterlife
bury skull and teeth
among the feathers of pillow
it is a graveyard for birds

you used to be   a bird

hide yourself during
the during
you can show your new body
to your mother
          in the aftermath

this hollow space is
where the spirit will reside

to be baptized by fire
you must first empty yourself
          of water

Self-Portrait as Rainbow Boy

Except for my teeth,
I am not a white thing.

My spectrum has its roots in disturbia,
with hues from yellowed bruises
to bloodshot eyes from crying too much.

True colors are said to be
the sweetest of enchantments,
but mostly they are heavier

than the weight of water.
I am good at truth, yes,

yet color and I do not bleed
at the same speed.

Cut yourself, then touch yourself.
It's a terrible song on repeat
all night.

Each cycle brings you closer
to the mouth of the drain.

From the prisma of the swirling,
I learn that you can still look pretty
in the middle of ruin.

To Worship Pollution

The wolves have done their worst;
we are done and have come
undone.

We are a bunch of verbs,
lying in a corner,
wrapped together in illusion,
listening to refrigerator hum,
      moonlight fracture,
      crickets by the river,
      loneliness.

We do not make love because
they are watching us & we have no love.

You touch my skin with
carcinogenic fingers –
      this. is. all. the. salvation.
      our. nakedness. can. buy.

This is what they have made of us.
We are all verb & no feeling, like
FUCK, SCREAM, HIDE, HATE, EVOLVE. FORGET.
Then REMEMBER. Then FORGET.

The moon is melting around us.
We have come undone, my tragedy.

We cannot make love.
A garden is blooming in the kitchen.

Picaresque

October rain can be cruel.
I get a head cold and touch myself
to thoughts of Marcus.
Things rush back –
memorabilia like collarbone hickeys
& bruised ribs
& the truth about love.
In my mind, his hands are all over my body;
in real life, moths are latching onto my hair.
I have theories, like
the earth doesn't spin unless two kids in love are kissing,
or
I don't love you like you love me.
If anyone is watching while we fuck,
we must look like musical notations,
complex constellations,
ancient runes.
His voice is calling birds into my bedroom,
hands stripping me as though I am a rosary.
We are a breed of divine abomination,
with the psychedelic hum of public nudity.
I have theories, like
why stay when you can go?
The earth isn't spinning anymore.
My head cold is making me insane.
The car tumbles like silence,
six times.
The sky is opening itself, a predator.
October rain can be blinding.
I die smiling & touching myself
to thoughts of Marcus.

Self-Portrait as a Study in Asphyxia

Prophecy is born on glossy pages.
The big bad wolf teaches that air
can tear down a home. Shelter,
reduced to termites & debris.
A dead body is whisked away.

Imagine.
A new place that is not home.
The Wizard of Oz teaches
that air can take you elsewhere
if you are already lost.

You are looking for a vehicle,
for names to give yourself.
Is there power in air,
or in making use of air?
In ghost stories, air is home.

Imagine.
A house's walls caving inward.
The colors run. An orchard is birthed
in the middle of ruination.
This place is called Eden.

Imagine.
A white rose in your mouth.
Stem in throat, thorns puncturing
the voice box. You sound like
an echo of someone else.

Epiglottis bursts & amen washes
over you. This is what rupture means.
You have no need to speak.

Imagine.
A fairy tale about suffocation.

The Ghost of Valentino

Sometimes, I wonder if I should have
come as a medium instead
of a fag.

That night of Christmas carols left me
haunted by red basketball jerseys &
impossible fevers,
New Musk & hip-hop.

I recall now:
the first of the ghosts was Valentino.
He had beautiful hair & soft hands.

Ghosts have followed me around since,
fragrant & inducing dusty love.
I hear them sing songs
about old bones & they always have

lisps. Hollow eyes too,
but they are soft.
I pretend they are singing to me.
I believe myself & then I curse myself.

These ghost boys, they make me hard
& the hauntings are hard
& the exorcisms are even
harder.

There is no use in seeing ghosts
if you cannot speak with them.

Tea With My Grandmother

my grandmother says I am thin &
I look too much like a waterfall
ribs covered in overgrown moss
a kind of lonely I was not raised to be

[silly boy   didn't your mother tell you
blue is a color for the dead]

yes   but how do you explain   yellow skin
turning green   is it true I was born
half dead

[you shouldn't listen to those nasty rumors
when you were born you were half alive
that is a different thing entirely]

isn't seventeen years enough to
tear me in two   why do you think
I can go on   I have never had
a name I can pronounce

[did you fall in love with someone]

yes   I did   it was similar to a shipwreck
my body became sea glass
why are we   talking   about this

[child   you cannot expect to stand still
when all the ocean does   is move   you have
to be a mew   or a version of yourself
that is plastic]

don't you see   I am already plastic
already a misadventure   how long before
the message dies   in its bottle

[you need to move on &
let go of the blood in your eyes]

you misunderstand   grandma   this is
just shrapnel under my skin   I know how
to let go   but not how to heal

[tear it off   nobody needs that much skin
what are you hiding from]

grandma   do you understand
I was in love with a boy

[I love the way   a seashore is continuous
why do you think   it is difficult
to figure you out]

so you know   I have crashed like a wave
countless times   because I want to be
known

[if you are in a haste   to eat hot soup
you will have no tongue   for when it cools]

sometimes   I need to slow down

[you know   I saw a fairy once
in a banana tree   I was nine
you remind me of her]

you've said that before   what
does that mean   this time

[milk teeth   I am saying you are like milk teeth
everything in you   is usually thrown away
except for   when it is kept]

On Fathers & Boiling Water

Papa faded away like dew in December.
The sorrow still dances in my hands sometimes.

I am gathering tears   for the day
when I turn to rain.

I pretend he would have looked
at my open body & called me beautiful.

I know he wouldn't; I'm lying to myself,
growing dizzy from steam & hopeless hope.

My stomach laughs at me,
ribcage groans in hunger.
You are cruel, please be quiet.

I'm sure there's nothing flawed in heaven;
the manna is sugar-free &
they have heterosexual sons &
perfectly grilled fish &

he probably has forgotten about me by now.
I really should learn to let go,

but I can't help thinking
I should have packed him a little box of salt
& my truth   & rainwater

for good luck. For a goodbye.
For good.

Self-Portrait as a Victim of Bug Spray

My sister sees my wings &
does not know they are attached to me.

I am standing on a glass bottle
in the living room, pretending to be

a piece of furniture. The infestation
feeds on wood; precious mahogany &

the fabric of family. She aims bow &
arrow at my back, the place where

my wings converge, seeing through them,
but not through me. White light

lances through my right lung &
suddenly I don't remember how to inhale.

Yellow dust is gushing from my mouth.
The mouth of the bottle topples into itself.

I am trapped within glass again.
The infestation fed on me before anything else.

Self-Portrait as Pussyboy

Your chair is carved from the same wood / as the chopping block. They are a pack / of hyenas, showing you that nothing is wolf enough / when it is outnumbered. / Their blood is thick with hate, laughter so loud / it may echo for all fourteen years of prison time. / They latch on to you with teeth & / do not let go. / A condom is filled with luminous dust & / dangled in your face. Some days, / survival is the only victory to fondle. / You do not have to be a wolf / to survive. You run off into the shadows, / tail between legs, but still breathing.

Kuebiko

i. There are aftershocks and the little boy wonders
what has happened this time.

ii. There was a man who put his mouth on my ear
and a man who grabbed my sister by her necklace.
A man who hit me until I bled.
A man who told me he loved me
& a man who pretended I was straight.
A man who shot up a nightclub.

> *The fairies are all over the floor.*
> *The holes in the walls illuminate*
> *the dust spinning in the silent aftermath.*
> *This place has not stopped being magical.*
> *The wings are still suspended in air.*

iii. There are men and there are aftershocks,
& there are times when they intersect.

iv. Hands are more terrifying than guns.
Hands are an earthquake.
They can heal but they hardly ever do.
Hands never feel confused when they are
choking the light out of young eyes.
Hands bleed when they hold flowers.

v. The little boy is afraid of hands,
& so he never holds them. He is also
afraid of men, but he wants to hold them.
The aftershocks never end &
his body remains riddled with light.

Ixora

The bees have come for scarlet petals.
The ixora bush is in full bloom.

*You can stuff dry flowers down my throat,
as long as they have no scent.*

I'm telling my sister that the wander
is holding me by my neck.

She's teaching me breathing exercises,
brewing chamomile.

I want to ask what to do
about the indigo in my eyes.

I'm sitting across from emptiness
in a bathtub. They're stoning

a gay boy & building a bonfire
around the ixora bush.

Breathing lessons are for those
who don't know how to live

underwater. *I'm doing as you said,
thinking of floating instead of drowning.*

I'm not crying, my face is leaking.
The ixora bush is withering, row by row.

Fleas

is a bitchboy still a bitchboy after he is dead
I mean to say
do you only discover kindness
after the faggot isn't listening anymore

where did the naughty little flea go
nobody know nobody know

depends   who is asking the question
I mean to say
who do you plan
to make the killer apologize to

the naughty little flea said
what a feast

she really is
a delicious beast

do knives know what they are used for
I mean to say
is the bitchboy also a bitchboy
to his mother

man   look at
all that cholesterol

how does a person define a spillage
I mean to say
does anyone cry
when a dead dog is buried

*The italicized words in the poem are lyrics taken from Miriam Makeba's
The Naughty Little Flea

Hope is a Box of Bees

after Sylvia Plath

I cross my broken fingers to make this wish,
that tree limbs protect me from the dragons

& malevolence. Beetles creep all over the couch.
The therapist says *trauma* is the word for it.

A fallen bird is turning into smoke.
I'm stirring my sweet tea, standing

in a blizzard of shedding leaves. I hope
my father is waiting for me at the forest edge

& I know he does not exist anymore.
The prescription pills are falling like rain.

Black Hoodie, Wolfboy, Heartache

It was the month of
photoshoots and
diagnoses:

your skull is shaped
like schizophrenia
and you need to rest.

He took your hand
and told you soy milk tastes
like indie music.

You crept into his jersey
after
midnight,

kissed his beard,
said: "he makes me remember
Valentino."

He loved you in a
hallucinogenic,
fucked you, aroused you.

You roused when the sun
laughed at you, then died
at midmorning.

Lonesome Bodies

A heron alights itself on the ground,
becomes fog. A man who wants

to love me without loving me
lays himself beside me & quotes

his grandfather, says *body no be firewood,*
which is to say he is feeling lonely

and human; which is to say he has never
seen a body contort into scream

& thick smoke, the merciless curl of naked wood.
He's calling my name in some kind

of sign language & I cannot see his hands,
do not know what he means.

I wonder if fog prevents a withered thing from
catching fire in the same way

it prevents sight. I wonder if he knows
how cold my bones are, how dehydrated &

how I stay because curling is for delicate things.
A different kind of bird is throwing itself from

the sky, bringing me to my body. I do not know what
names he has for me. I am calling him a cloud—

he is clueless as every cloud is,
letting me let go of him. I become

a fog, too & then I fade away.

Learning to Float

Both water & air can float
a morning-bird's feather.

Beneath shimmering flux,
there is a testament to

a folktale other than this
angled survival. The mirage

of surface is a body uncharted.
The sea says she is red

in more places than you know &
a bird is hardly ever a swimmer.

The fact of the unseen is
also a witch's covenant.

A mirror, also a knife.

Even the Birds

I come from a hot country with magic / woven in its threads. In December, / Sahara dust envelops everything. / It looks like a disintegration / that we have earned. I have / blue feathers at the center of my palms & / at the base of my spine & too often, / I dream of snow. To make an angel in the snow / is to carve something divine out of heathen bones. / The December in my ribs begins / with dust seeping & settling. Then the cold / fills up all the cracks / with a loneliness that smells like old paper & / sweet mold. Snow is falling in my ribs & / still, I wish for winter. There must be moments / when even the birds want to be birds.

TFW You Are Just A Roadmap

the light is tired and the sky quiets
into a dusk that feels private

enough for him to strip down
to bare skin and settle

in the parts of us that are river enough
to wash over him

in the seclusion of flow
asking him not

to become water because it hurts
to constantly be water

and not be able to move
he has come

past the rocky sections of our bodies &
what is left is the green

& the restraint it requires
to love a cartographer

who thinks we are not the desert
who looks at us and sees

the outline of wings that belong
to extinct birds

who thinks of us as a call to prayer
not seeing

that he has not yet found
a place that looks enough like home

Stillbirth, Yemoja

In Yoruba, there is no translation
for mismatch and no word for membrane.

Skin translates to flesh translates to body.
A person is bound to make them heavy.

The cohesion is an only friend.
I am the kind of man who is a feather.

I spill myself and come unstuck.
Whole makes parts. Parts do not make whole.

Whole is missing something.
The cohesion does not know me—

the kind of man who wants to be
the kind of woman who bears children

that sound like birds
when they cry.

There is a word for rebirth
but it connotes the aftermath

of a sticky death. A body is bound
so it sinks when it drowns.

I am unsure that I have enough names
to be something other than what I am.

The Bodies of Dead Boys

my boyfriend   is a mortician
the kind that sits next to   crows
enjoying the odor of departure
the coming   and the going
I am unfamiliar but he claims
to know me   I sell my body to him
for information   tell me
what you know of me   am I truly
a river   or is that a hallucination too
is it normal to talk to shovels
and ask them   to be gentle
I'm sorry   how did we meet again
something about bicycles   wasn't it
about going round   about brakes
he claims I am not an ending
I try to prove myself   a group
of crows is a murder   a group
of shovels is a pile   a pile
of bodies is the pilgrimage where scorpio hands
teach me   to open my bones
and reveal insects and marrow
I strip myself   he thinks it is
about sex and preservation
I call myself   a half-dead thing
this romance   my embalmment
he claims to be able to make me trickle
I tell him I love him   in a wounded way

Self-Portrait as a Safe House by the Sea

after Peter LaBerge

Reality check: my mouth still tastes / like salt on the surface of a prayer. A hand / is the adorning around my throat, the sides / of which were made to cleanse the impure. Because I am / void & because I am vast & because / I am ocean. A hand is a ghost, / the one around my throat. My hand holds a ghost / itself because my body is the haunted / house. A hand slams a door. My mouth is / a door. My mouth is closed & my mouth / is empty & my mouth is vast. / The window lets in a beam of light. My / teeth are beams of light. My mouth is also window & / my body is open sea & I am the reflection I do not / see in it. The light is floating. The water / is floating, too.

ACKNOWLEDGMENTS

These poems originally appeared, sometimes in different forms, in the following publications.

> *Vagabond City:* "Black Hoodie, Wolfboy, Heartache"
> *Spy Kids Review:* "Ixora"
> *HIV Here and Now:* "Self-Portrait As Pussyboy" (appeared as "No Homo")
> *Figroot Press:* "Self-Portrait As A Child Who Isn't Yours"
> *Glass: A Journal of Poetry:* "The Bodies of Dead Boys"
> *Wildness:* "Stillbirth, Yemoja"

Thanks to Betty Godson, for reading every single draft of this book, and who stuck with me through all of the self-doubt and cold feet. Thanks to Tomisin Adebisi, for her unwavering faith in me. Thanks to Heritage, whose optimism carried me through most days.

My gratitude to Robert Carr, for his perspective, feedback, and his help in shaping this book into what it has become, and to Stephen Zerance, for his invaluable review of the early work. Thanks to Anthony Frame, for the endless support. Thanks to Alexis Bates and Jasmine Cui, from the other side of the world.

Thanks to everyone at Indolent Books.

Thanks to my family and the wonderful friends I am lucky to have.

Special thanks to Michael Broder, my publisher, my mentor, my friend. Thank you, Michael. I love you, Michael.

ABOUT THE AUTHOR

Logan February was born in Anambra, Nigeria, in 1999 and grew up in Ibadan, Oyo. He is a singer-songwriter, a poet, a procrastinating novelist, and a very average psychology major at the University of Ibadan.

He is a queer and happy-ish Nigerian owl who likes pizza & typewriters, and he lives in Ibadan, where he is lucky enough to have the greatest friends.

He is co-editor-in-chief of *The Ellis Review*, and is the author of two chapbooks, *Painted Blue with Saltwater* (Indolent Books) & *How to Cook a Ghost* (Glass Poetry Press). Please say hello @loganfebruary.

ABOUT INDOLENT BOOKS

Indolent Books is a small poetry press founded in 2015 and operating in Brooklyn, N.Y. Indolent was founded as a home for poets of a certain age who have not published a first collection. But the mission of the press is broader than that: Ultimately, Indolent publishes books the editors care about. The main criteria are that the work be innovative, provocative, risky, and relevant. Indolent is queer flavored but inclusive and maintains a commitment to diversity among authors, artists, designers, developers, and other team members. Indolent Books is an imprint of Indolent Arts Foundation, Inc., a 501(c)(3) nonprofit charity founded in January 2017.

www.ingramcontent.com/pod-product-compliance
Lightning Source LLC
Chambersburg PA
CBHW021453080526
44588CB00009B/830